Growth

Tiffany LaShay

ROYSTON
Publishing

BK Royston Publishing
P. O. Box 4321
Jeffersonville, IN 47131
502-802-5385
http://www.bkroystonpublishing.com
bkroystonpublishing@gmail.com

© Copyright – 2020

All Rights Reserved. No part of this book may be reproduced, stored in a retrieval system, or transmitted by any means without the written permission of the author.

Cover Design: Gad by Elite Cover Designs

ISBN-13: 978-1-951941-26-0

Printed in the United States of America

All Glory to my Lord and Savior,

Jesus Christ,

For implanting these words inside of

my soul and

Allowing them to grow, so that

others are able to

Pick them from my garden.

My children,

Maurice, Carter, and Alexander,

This is for you.

I attribute to you

My growth

As a mother,

As a woman.

For both of my grandmothers,

Betty Whetstone and Audrey Hinton,

Thank you for

Your words of encouragement and

Instilling your creativity.

Dad,

Thank you for giving me

Your eyes and for always

Seeing the things that I could not.

Mom,

Thank you for

Giving me your ears and

Listening.

Jason Brooks,

Thank you for

Giving me our three sons.

We planted three of the most

Precious flowers in a garden

I tend with grace.

Nathaniel Ward,

I must admit

I was unsteady.

Now I am focused

And ready.

I have stepped from comfort

and onto platforms

to display my artistry

to be a visionary.

I see myself in 20/20

With great precision.

You know that I have

A very unique and special gift.

You tell me what I need

To unwrap my presence.

I appreciate you

For encouraging me

to speak louder

in places

where I didn't bring a match.

You struck the essence

to spark the light

You attribute to my luminescence.

Within my gift

is yours:

A present divinely created

in the spirit of

Love, trust, and friendship

held by truth.

You are a blessing.

Thank you.

Big ups to

Chris "Deep Sea" Rice

For encouraging me to

"Keep Spitting"

Robin Garner and

Lance G. Newman II,

Thanks to you both

For setting the stages

where I have been able

To speak my peace.

For my readers,

I grew up

With the aspiration of being tall.

I must admit that

I fell short.

Table of Contents

Acknowledgements	iii
Golden Chocolate	3
Granny Green Thumb	7
Deep	10
Youth	13
Roots	16
In Between Breaths	17
Bliss	19
Clouds	22
3 Headed Monster	24
In Between the Breaths	27
Rib Tips	36
Grow On, Girl	41
I Am Arose	43
Vessel	45
Madonna	49

Choice	53
Playground	62
Mr. Write Back	65
Rising Sons (Haiku)	70
Son's Flower	71
The Best Gift	73
Heart to Heart	74
Sincerest Apologies	76
"Lion to a Lying Queen"	77
Warrior	78
Leaving	80
I Am Arose (Haiku)	82
Wedged	83
"Laundry"	85
Hope	88
As We	89
"Inspired By"	93
Engrafted (Haiku)	94
Good Rising (Haiku)	95

Peace by Piece 96

Growth is conceived through prideful roots being tugged and pulled together over the course of time. In our growth we hold onto the spiritual gems we have collected along the way.

Golden Chocolate

His dreads

Spread love

Her voice

Sprinkles grace

One is golden

One is chocolate

Two of the things

I love

The way their poetry tastes

Delicate

Like Ferrero Rocher

Yet richer

And so much deeper

Resonating

From the mind

To the tongue

Purifying my lungs

With this gift

They're sharing with me

An incredible presence

The transparency is

A blessing

I admire their essence

Raising questions

Facilitating

Life lessons that aren't taught in schools

But once a month

On a Sunday

I get them

I love this

I love y'all

Robin, you keep showing up

Lance, you keep spreading love

I appreciate the opportunities

You provide

For the Black community

It's Golden

It's beautiful

It's rich

It's sweet

It's rooted in hard labor

It brings us relief

It's chocolate

Golden Chocolate

Granny Green Thumb

Everything she touched managed to bloom

She could make anything grow

No matter how rotted the root

She had that special touch

To make everything better

Sometimes she overdid it

Being a gardener extraordinaire

She worked so well with her hands

God blessed her with an incredible pair—

Whether it was to pat you on the back

Or to give you a swat

It was out of love

Something she never forgot

A birthday

Graduation

Morning worship

The pants that needed a hem

A play

Doctor's visits

Hair appointments

Spare change that you might have needed for the bus

Or to give you a ride

If you needed her

She was there

To plant the words

Craftily sown

As the many flowers she nurtured at home

Deep

We call him Deep

Because his words

Hold depth

To the sound of

But Cheats

Getting smacked

With his dreadlocks

Flowing like his lines

Illuminated by his phone

Snapping everywhere he goes

Shows after shows

From C. to Sea

His pen is still like water

Verses rippling

Through the vibes

Of church

Voices is where I heard him first

Sitting in that chair at open mic

Expressing his thoughts

Through the spirit of virtue

His waves get deeper

Even though he's got his mane locked

In poetic prowess like a Mansa

Intertwining metaphors and similes

Springing from each coil

With ease

He puts on at performances

In between Lance and Robin G.

A man whose talent

Is pure and clear

Like the ocean

Lines flowing

Over likes and sees

He's forming verses

Mountain-like waves overseas

That's why we call him

Deep

Youth

In the nineties

I was a child

Blowing bubbles

Running through sprinklers

Getting into stuff

Making business

With things that weren't mine

I have to own

The memories

Not always pleasant

But, I kept them

Without them

I wouldn't be clothed

I'd be naked in

Naiveté

Never growing

To understand

The concept of

Youth

When I was full

Of anxiety and rushing to grow up

Now I'd rather sit

Reflecting

Good and bad days

Instead of dying like a slave

I'd rather pass

Like the time

Going with old age

Roots

Sturdy limbs strengthen

the trees flourishing from deep

lies sewn in fertile soil.

In Between the Breaths

Bliss

He grasped my hand

As if he were entrusting me

With the most beloved possession

I felt his palm slide onto mine

Eyes peering into his

Dark brown irises

Holding glimpses of myself

I gave him a vignette

Of my love

Deep and insatiable

We came to

Our mutual attraction

A titillating caress

Captures anxiety

Within a shroud

Of vulnerability and truth

Remaining in the awkward position

You cannot flex

For the sake of

Losing it

We're both

Gasping for breath

Soft whispers request more

As we switch positions

My body atop your

Eyes glancing at mine

Toes raising from the floors

Pleasure was inside of me first

Then it came

To be yours

Clouds

Puffy white dreams soft like linen I rest my head on, contemplating my day, do I want to start it as I punch in to receive my key, I think I want to leave and never return, but they're waiting on me to do a job for eleven dollars above free, but I need it through times tough like firm pillows jobs are great for support and bad for your face, I need a soft plush one to rest in when times get rough from behind the butt, knees to chest like a tornado tuck, these clouds will spin you regardless of what you're into, there's something fascinating about being overtaken, lifted and shook, you're lost within the formations between His creation of blue and white illuminated by the sun shining upon you in a nutritious orange, you're hydrated with its kiss blown by the breeze playing hide and go seek within the trees squirrels get their nuts and drop their seeds like animals they are, not equivalent to us sitting on this bench, earbuds in looking up and down the street for the next bus, I must have missed the last one, although, I'm enjoying my day as it wastes away, sharing jokes to pass the time as lightness begins to fade into the clouds as they become gray transforming into a deeper purple, dying within the night, there's always a prayer to be requested, as we bow our heads, asking God to bring back the morning light and thanking him for his blessings.

3 Headed Monster

It's impossible to let you in knowing that he's behind the door waiting for me to come into this apartment meant for two. It cannot be us three and it kills me because in a way I do love him because he expresses everything to me and not just what it's going to be or should be, he tells me how it is… If I'm going to sacrifice a relationship that brought kids for one that brought noncommittal trust looming in the pit of my stomach aches because I'm tempted to go with my gut, despite having other feelings because he's willing to forgive and I'm not willing to forego a situation that has been so-so, somewhat hating the fact that I divulged so much I needed to vent and you weren't there to breathe the air left when you left now I'm fanning myself with dry tears that won't fall because I'm the happiest I've ever been around him.

I'm speaking of you and sometimes it is ill, although the words remain true. It's hard loving two people, he reminds me a lot of you, even though he possesses a deeper complexion and smacks when he eats food, it's something I bypass like how I'm feeling with you knowing my intention of making this move from a pawn to a king is a complicated transition. I can't decipher between him or you. I slide back a couple of squares in fear that I might lose something that's still missing, a void yet to be filled with awe and chilling thrills when you pull the hair at the nape of my neck, a tug reminiscent of a thrusting, passionate push into the wall, I'm stumbling into kisses that should belong to another missus and I'm bound to be if only we could be joined together and not limited to these vacant rooms.

You see, there's beauty in everything. I don't need a wedding ring from him or you. Even though I want you. I need myself and I can't help to shake the fact I find remnants of that within you, too. You have helped me to acknowledge my truth scattered across the bed, accompanied by three heads gnawing at our sanity, gnashing all humanity to unleash the beast from a box that I willingly opened and now it's ever-present.

In Between the Breaths

I.

Air filling my lungs

Feeling the crisp crunch of leaves

Wrinkled with old age

II.

Fountains sprinkle cold

Splashes of water in the

Faces masked in hatred

III.

Hovering over

Our ears clogged with bales tied like

Freedom domes the sky

IV.

Burning arenas

Felt in red hearts ready to

Burst through Spirit's flow

V.

In open churches

When a man confesses sins

Pouring out like rain

VI.

Dried away like youth

Full of dry bones only two

Rejuvenated

VII.

By His light shining

Upon them in darkest times

He weathers storms

VIII.

Lightning rods bolt

Piercing purple reign strikes in

Thunder claps hitting

IX.

Windows hard in pane

After the pain came to us

Our door unhinged

X.

We were never touched

Marked with an X possessed by

Holy presence

XI.

Traveling in pairs

To share our blessing as Christ

Avowed through Saul

XII.

Persevering through

The account of Job and Dan

Possessing strength

XIII.

Remains of loyal hands

In hands better grasping fruit

Eve bit first to quench

XIV.

Her thirst for desire

Scorns us all succumbing to

The fall of a man

XV.

It was in God's plan

To permeate his purpose within

Us

XVI.

To restore nations

To rightful owners writing

Words proclaimed by Him

XVII.

That we are His sons

And daughters who were spread 2

Cross the seas and winds

XVIII.

Beings driven into

Lands where they do not speak 2 us

Language lingers in the desert

XIX.

Acknowledge us as

Kings and queens created in-

Divisible by 1

XX.

Darker skinned nation

Rooted and ingrained

Deep as brown soil

We are rich as stolen spoils

Rib Tips

Spread from his loins

Broken off into a slender curve

I am the backbone

Taking shape

Holding place

To support you

Without me

The flavor is withheld

As the sauces becomes a puddle

In a tin foil pan

When you could have

Grasped me in your hands

I'm that delicate dish

Being preserved

On the backburner

You tried to hide me

Knowing that your family's

Meddlesome noses had to

Take a peek

A whiff

To see what was inside

Smoke rose

Filling the air

Aromatic honey barbecue

As you fix your plate

I'm right there

Clinging to your lanky self

Putting some meat on your bones

I've got you licking your lips

A piece of me is in between

Your teeth bite the tangy sweet

Until there's nothing left

But tips

Discarded in the same carryout box

I came in

With the collard greens, macaroni and cheese, and tall pink lemonade

All washed down with a slice of melon

I eat on the stoop

Knees to chest

Water dripping to my feet

In between the seeds

I'm licking my lips

To taste the sweet

Until there's nothing left

But the skin of this gourd

Then I lick my fingers

To remember how it felt

Now I'm craving more

Grow on, Girl

You cannot assemble a broken puzzle. Why are you trying to fix him? You can mend tattered pieces with tape, but not even a Band-Aid is able to conceal the damage that has been created. Why are you so adamant on proving your existence to him? He sees you. The problem is he cannot see himself, which is where it lies.

Gather your belongings and let him fix his own mess. He shouldn't have invited you to play knowing that he doesn't have a complete set. You're wasting time. Pack up your things and all that you brought and place them in the box to help him out.

Your kindness will not be forgotten, but your presence needs to fade.

I am Arose

Vessel

In order for our light to shine

We must be transparent

So that others will

See through us

To receive the beam of hope

Raised within our bodies' rays

We are luminescent of change

Reflected through our lives

Juxtaposed, yet in symmetry

Split images are pieced together

Creating a beautiful mosaic

Like stained glass windows

Within temples

Guarded as safe havens

We are protected within ourselves

Through Him

We acknowledge the similarities

We learn to live with our differences

We are not perfect

We are more like salt

Just a sprinkle is required

To appease one's faith

We come in like grain

Sifted through channels

Across the Euphrates

Along a journey

Up and through Sinai

We parted ways

Guided by his staff

We follow His word

Blindly listening to His voice

All we could hear were the birds

Somewhere in the wilderness

We fell and were supported by

Engrafted branches

Rooted specifically for us

To latch onto

We move on through

Despite being previously led astray

We continue to seek Him

To find our way

We hold hands

Blindly led by faith

He showers us with rain

Pouring out like a vessel

Sifting through

To change

Madonna

Pregnant with a child

Yet to be born in father

Less homes below

Poverty lines strict

Ending commodities

No longer than eyes

Lashing out when they

Have been cut from programs aired

Through a channel's white noise

It sounded alright 'til'

We established our own dreams

In communities of our own

Where our own people

Conduct business by hands

2 be hands exchanged

Between our own people

Entrepreneurs who demonstrate changes

In our own people

Raising fists

4 and against our own people

Committing challenges

Driving Hagar out

Never admitting the Sarah

Within our own people

We were descended from

Potters that were stolen for

Trade amongst our own

People disown people

We should gather to ignite power

Within our own people

To spark a new life

Created 4 our own people

Driven through strife

We sacrifice for our own people

Choice

Thank you for the offer

But I've got this

I've been watching my mother

Tote her own bags

For twenty-eight years

She may have stumbled

She never fell down though

She started wearing sneakers

 Instead of heels

A single mother doesn't have enough time to trot

There's always an errand

You must run

Get it done

Your children don't need to see another incomplete

The task is often bitter

But, glancing at those smiles

Provide a lightness in your feet

You can't help tilting your head back

Letting the coils bounce free and

Not bound by a scarf

Or the hat you've been wearing

Eight hours

You're at home now

A place of satisfaction

Because you're the one who built it

Its foundation is a blessing

It's not perfect

Every home has cracks

That just means it was destined for the journey and

It settled over time

White walls painted

Purple and bright green

Two choice colors of mine

We're all given a choice

So, make a decision

Sometimes I have to stop

To think about it

I am tired

I appreciate the kind gesture

No thank you

It's just one more block

Besides, you don't know me

I don't know you

I speak because my mother spoke first

It wasn't an invitation

Just an act of common courtesy

That bewildered your amazement

We're not like most city folk

I guess

Maybe it's the Whetstone and Hinton

Between us

That makes us so close

Great friends and diligent workers

Just don't push our limits

Because when we're through

Everyone will notice that

Something wasn't right

Always smiling, staying late,

Lending an extra hand

Ticking a twenty fifth hour

Because the kids need new clothing

Forgetting about yourself

Wearing the Buddy's with a rip in them

To make due

You don't fret

Because you find contentment

Knowing that your children

Have you and you have them

Hearts beating rhythmically

That boom, boom, boom

Within our chests

Flows through my veins

Like the poetry you've instilled

The ink from this pen

Drips at its own will and

You all chose to support me

I'm grateful

Truly blessed

You didn't have to

Yet you chose to

We all have a choice

To love and give and share and

Love you

For encouraging me to utilize my voice

Doing what's best for me and my children

Never straying too far from his word

Believing that we can do all things

Despite the circumstances

You pray anyway and

We've all been kept

In love

It was His choice and

We've got it

The option to choose

Overcoming obstacles with

Neo-soul

Jazz

Nineties rhythm and blues

Giovanni and Langston Hughes

I grab a pen and paper

To sit and reminisce

To show my appreciation

It's my choice to give you this

Playground

It's amazing how at such a young age

Boys possess the concept of conquering

Fighting over who is

Going to be king

They each view it in themselves

I don't step in

Nor do they ask me

It's not my place

Sometimes you have to

Allow them to roam

Testing their limits

Stumbling and falling down

Now, they may need a little push

And you're behind them

To give that

Support

Or a reprimand

In either situation

You are there

To push the swing

To catch him as he slides

Or to deter him from playing in mulch

That hour or two of playtime

Matters the most

You were there

On the playground

Now he's grown

Taller and strong enough

To rock climb

He's looking down

With pride

Mr. Write Back

I think he's Mr. Write

Though, I'm not quite sure

He's more than a muse

Of thoughts and love that lures

Ink between stationery sheets

Closed inside

He's the only one

Who possesses the key

To my secret journal and

Reads my poems pleasantly

When we ride

He provides insight

Requesting more

He begins instantly and ending silently

…

Breathless ellipses

Affirm admiration

He chuckles and strokes his goatee

In a moment of contemplation

Remembering those times

Everything was just fine

It felt like I was his and he were mine

We've shared multiple nights

Caught between the boundary

Of friendship and romance

Not knowing which to choose

I was strutting around town

Too small for my shoes

My vision had been altered

The pen faltered and its grip I would lose

Somehow,

He brought that light back

He brought that write back

To give me assurance

To get me through it

To send me snaps

To uplift me

When I haven't begun to make the bed

He smooths out the wrinkles ironed in low-count linen thread

I smile

Each day he's in my presence

Even when he's not

He's drawn somewhere

Between my ears and above my nose

Releasing all these feelings

I thought were frozen

Ice melts

Absolving the stickiness

Honey drizzled

Across my breasts

Warm nipples erect

Penetrating

A gap between teeth

Is an opening for me

Rising Sons (Haiku)

Seeds sown in our love

tended with grace and water

sprout in proper time.

Son's Flower

He gave me a flower

From the tree planted

In our backyard

He told me

It was for love

The simplest bud

Nothing fancy

It was in bloom

Something I can't recall

Treasuring from you and

It made my soul smile

Having received such love and

It was from my own

Child

The Best Gift

I never cared for

The jewelry

I was not fascinated by

The shine

All I wanted

Was a moment of

Your time

Wrapped in penmanship

To display the effort

To express how you felt

From a place

Deep within

Heart to Heart

I know that you love me. What bothers me is the uncertainty shadowing my heart when I try to say it, too. My mouth says the words, but my eyes look on through. A part of me holds onto the memories yet my feet desire to move on to grasp the purpose of a life built anew. I'm searching for myself. I became lost when I tried to escape fated love because I was afraid of the former.

I'm writing this to say I'm sorry if I cherished him more and treated you like less. I'm sorry if I granted him access to parts of me that you've never seen. I'm sorry if I allotted time for him to fill your spot. I'm sorry if these ifs aren't really ifs because certain wishes were fulfilled. I'm sorry that I didn't listen to your concerns. I'm sorry I never told you what it was because it was something that happened just because and now I'm drowning in feelings deep enough to become buried, covered in ash until the smoke clears. I'm just to lie in a bed of emptiness until I'm able to make it right.

Sincerest Apologies

Justifying our problems doesn't solve anything unless we can gather our own faults and acknowledge that we both have contributed to the shift that has made our journey rocky yet, somehow, we still manage to remain friends who occasionally leave to better focus on themselves and, of course, the relationship is going to change as people do.

Never stay the same, because in order for us to grow together we have to experience pain, because without it there wouldn't be any healing to this wound as it would forever be a scar that never got its chance to breathe.

"Lion to a Lying Queen"

How can I be your queen if I cannot see your crown? Let alone the fact that mine has yet to be obtained. How can we succeed in a proper dynasty without our royal attire? Unbefitting to the throne we must go on, banished from the pride lands that we once called home as we outcast ourselves to be trapped in our own egos. We cannot return until we have come to terms.

Warrior

Women shouldn't dim each other's light because one woman chose to step outside of the box and climb on top

Ayesha, I admire women like you who are willing to acknowledge that marriage isn't perfect, and demonstrate effective communication between husband and wife

Reaffirming that love is a choice and that we should all be willing to address it as our own

Right to speak on

Insecurities developed in the lack of attention

Others view it as disrespect, though, I believe that Steph understood despite being upset and he remains loyal

Reminding us that love is a 50/50 partnership and that a man cannot complete me and that I must possess the other half.

Leaving

Maybe it's best I leave

Because I don't know

 how much longer I'll be able to stay

Maybe it's best I leave

The kisses at the door

Locked behind you as I walk down the hall

Maybe it's best I leave

The day's greetings in morning ellipses until your head begins to rise

Maybe it's best I leave

My feelings inside, maybe, I won't feel this pain

Maybe it's best I leave

Unreciprocated love in the empty frame

Maybe it's best I leave

Maybe it's best you leave

Me alone to love myself with pride

Maybe the answer is

Yes

I am Arose (Haiku)

Like a flower in

between cracks of pavement I

blossom in the sunlight.

Wedged

Nothing can come between us. He is a wedge and as a wedge he has given me support. When you weren't accessible to me I did seek comfort in his arms because he knew how to console me at the time, and feelings were able to be touched by fingers laid on my shoulder as a friend who gives you a pat on the back; however, I empathize and understand where you're coming from because I've been there before I met you, never knowing the definition of love.

It was just something to say in moments of good times that were coming to their terse in the form of byes, although, I'd like to know how it feels to say hello when we rise together in the face of the sun straining our eyes to see each other when the morning comes, making breakfast for the children and getting them ready for school.

He is a wedge and as a wedge he has given me support which makes me a better fit to express these feelings to you that in hindsight I didn't believe you would get so I hid them, and I admit, it made it harder for me and you, and I don't regress over past decisions.

I hope that you can find it in your heart to forgive me and believe nothing can come between us. He is just someone who did.

"Laundry"

Caught between an epiphany of déjà vu I don't know what to do or who to call, Him or you. I thought that I was through this, both songs suggest me leaving you, and I'm caught in the box trying to move this, showing little strength, barely moving it, and you keep coming back into my changing life, revolving as I'm evolving, spinning my wheels turning like a chariot, I cannot carry it due to a lack of strength. I do not have the arms of a porter nor a carter.

I cannot bear this unwearable load, hung out to dry, heavy as wet clothes, I'm lingering in my robe, cloaked and self-loathed, basking in a cautious heat, sun-stroked attire that other women aspire as men perspire because they are too weak to try it on themselves.

Their load is too heavy and delicate to be washed in a cycle with light fluff and hot water, yet, there's a coolness that has been permanently pressed within its fabric to avoid ruining the stitching of this quilt, patch worked over the years it has been through many hands, of many colors, sorted and piled to be laundered and made clean for others, to lie on and wrap their bodies into, absorbing the heat providing warmth to a body freezing from coldness that no bodies have ever used for shelter, like beds in rooms with blankets brought in woven baskets that we carry over our heads.

Traveling for miles until we can see our own trips, we take years sojourning for our presence, going back and preserving a lot for future presents, wrapped and woven tight like baskets we carry on our heads, possessing the strength of a porter and a carter we bear this heavy load in a delicate cycle, permanently pressed.

Hope (Haiku)

Stranded in a drought

lacking sufficient water

embrace your own light.

As We

Sheer material

Covers her eyes

As she walks

Down a path of

Roses laid

To cover

Her former self

In the wake of

Anew

Life

Being submerged

Into

The sun encompasses the moon

Lightness of day and night

Creates magic

Among the room

Surrounded by love and secret jealousy

Onlookers wait for me

To lock eyes with my groom

He removes

My veil of vulnerability

To discover a woman

Remains contrite in spirit

Through years of drought

Showered in reign

We are joined to be

Bound by a cord of three strings

His and mine guided by an invisible hand

We each touch

To reminisce fond memories

Overshadowing times thick

I glance at him

Through clouds

Of happily provoked tears

To see he has his own

To see he is a reflection of me

To see I am a part of him

To see the words I read as a child

To see us live them now

To see us love them like they love we

To see our noses touch and agree

To see I do's in exchange for

Yes, we

As we place these rings on our fingers

To symbolize the eternal circle

Holding us together

"Inspired By"

New York native, bred in Black excellence, possessing an essence reflecting the sun, you shine naturally

Affirming the notion that we were created in his image as kings and queens

Through preserved passages of paths paved in history

Haitians emancipated themselves

Aspiring for better opportunities of success

Never doubting their ability

Inspiring others to keep the same

Energy vibrating and ringing in positivity as you

Live life on your own terms

Engrafted Branch (Haiku)

Rooted in support

held on limbs of barking truth

His love never breaks.

Good Rising (Haiku)

Day comes in mourning

rain cleansing anew land for

flowers to blossom.

Peace By Piece

Sleepless nights, pens marking sheets streaked with ink unable to be removed to prove the point in manifesting a collection of stationery pages stacked and crumbled within corners of lives no longer arbitrary.

You put that mess together to create something beautiful, unique, and divine. What was once junk lies in the belly of the beast as I rip this piece so that you can better eat this peace. I'm deading all negativity to keep this piece within my heart and I wish that we would end the violence causing the disarray within this peace meant to open our eyes so that we can see each other to reunify this piece.

Peace.

www.ingramcontent.com/pod-product-compliance
Lightning Source LLC
LaVergne TN
LVHW022323080426
835508LV00041B/2386